THE RAT PACK OF HOLLYWOOD VISITS THE STATE FAIR

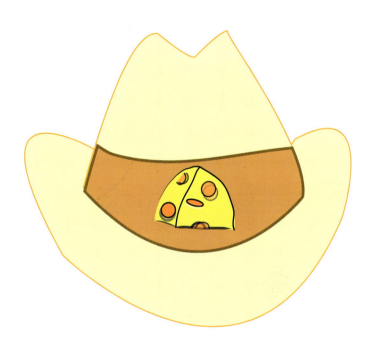

WRITTEN & ILLUSTRATED BY MICHAEL HOUBRICK

**Dedicated to God. Thank you for the talents
you gave to make this rat dream become a reality.**

Copyright © 2013 By Mr. Brick Publishing
All rat rights reserved.
No design, text, or artwork in this book may be reproduced
or used in any form or by any means - including but not
limited to:
electronic recording or by any information storage
and retrieval system, without permission
in writing from the author or publisher.
Inquiries should be addressed to
Mr. Brick Publishing
info@mr-brick.com
Printed in the USA by Jostens Printing & Publishing

Library of Congress Cataloging-in-Publication Data
Houbrick, Michael
The Rat Pack of Hollywood Visits The State Fair
Written & Illustrated by Michael Houbrick
Summary: The celebrity rats from Hollywod visit a state fair
and Randoon thinks he is the star attraction.
[1. Rats-Children's Fiction. 2. Picture Book 3. Humor]
Library of Congress Control Number (LCCN): 2012916777
ISBN 13: 978-0-9882523-3-2

There are many great things about the end of summer and the beginning of fall.

~~Leaves falling and~~ cheese
changing colors...

Rat hands down, the best thing about fall is the state fair!

This fall, The Rat Pack of Hollywood are super excited about going to the State Fair.

To no other rat's surprise, Randoon's favorite part of going to the fair is eating all of the fair food.

RANDOON'S TOP 5 FAVORITE FAIR FOODS

1. Deep Fried Cheese
2. Cheese-On-A-Stick
3. Corn Dog with Cheese
4. Soft Pretzel & Cheese
5. Cheese Covered Funnel Cakes

Randoon + Cheese = Love

Randoon knew that Ana would scold him for wanting to eat sugary fair food.

Bernie gathered up all of the rats in the bus and they headed for the fairgrounds.

Bernie is the rat in charge. It seems like he might be spoiling the fun, but he just wants what is best for the group.

"Leave your ego and cheese at the door!"

Bernie

Once again, The Rat Pack of Hollywood's appearance was sold out!

Lil' Jojo was hard at work rehearsing for the big show.

And so were all of the other rats... except Randoon!

?

Randoon thought it was the perfect time for a quick nap.

The Rat Post

Weather Partly Sunny

The most widely circulated rodent newspaper on the planet

COMEDIAN RANDOON STEALS THE SHOW

State Fair Opened Today

RANDOON

18

And the blue ribbon winner for the best home made apple pie is...

There was a sign that said, "FREE CARNIVAL RIDES TODAY!"

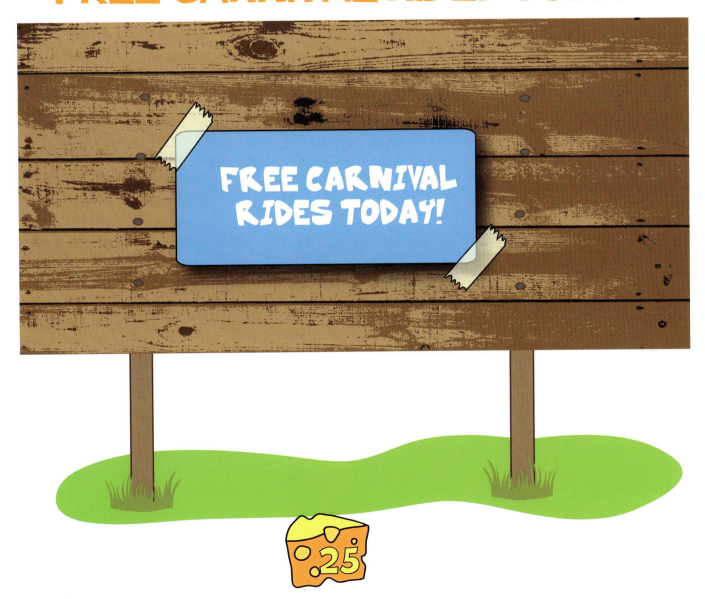

"Hey Randoon, free food, free carnival rides, a blue ribbon... is this your best day ever?" asked Sunny.

"Yes, and you'd better pinch me because I think I'm dreaming!" replied Randoon.

"Hey, what's going on? Where are all of my blue ribbons? And where are the stuffed animals I won on the midway? Why aren't you all wearing cowboy hats?" questioned a very sleepy Randoon.

"What are you talking about? When we got here you went and bought some cotton candy and a milkshake. Then, you laid down in that barn for a nap. That was four hours ago."

"It's time for our show now!" scolded Bernie.

"Country music? Now that's funny. You're such a silly rat, Randoon."

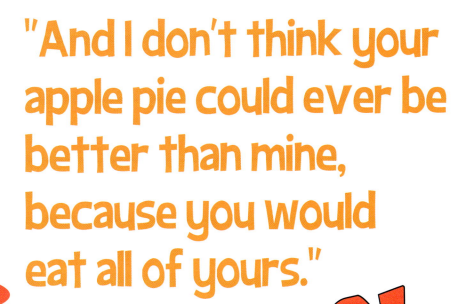

"And I don't think your apple pie could ever be better than mine, because you would eat all of yours."

ZING!